"Offering It Up"

for

Souls and the World

William Timmerman, PhD

"Offering It Up"

for

Souls and the World

2017

Penshop Publishing

San Antonio, Texas

William Timmerman, PhD

Table of Contents

Introduction

When I was a little boy in a Catholic grade school, I first heard the expression "offering it up" from a nun right before Lent. The words were connected to something called a "mission box." It was the same size as a Barnum's animal crackers box that has a picture of a circus animal maybe a lion in a cage on the side. The mission box had a picture of starving children somewhere in the world. On the top of the box next to the slot for inserting coins were the words "My Offering". On the way to school I would search for any lost money on the ground and would celebrate finding something if it was only a penny. Feeling around under padded chairs and the sofa in our house often resulted in finding some loose change. Many times I would use my milk money for school to put it instead in my mission box.

The "offering it up" is to God. It is an outward and upward sacrifice presented to Him. It was common practice for pagans to offer up sacrifices to their gods in idol worship. In the Old Testament, Abraham was ready to sacrifice his son Isaac as proof of his faith and obedience to God. At the last moment he was told to stop because he was tested and found faithful. The ultimate sacrifice was Jesus' offering up of himself throughout all the preliminary torture and finally his crucifixion for the salvation of mankind. In the Catholic Eucharistic celebration, the priest offers the bread and wine during the part of the Mass called the Offertory.

One of the prayers is, "We offer to you God of glory and majesty, this holy and perfect sacrifice; the bread of life and the cup of eternal salvation." Another prayer is "Through your goodness, Lord, we have this bread and wine to offer, the fruit of the earth and the work of human hands. They will become our spiritual food." The Offertory also includes a collection from the parishioners for almsgiving to the poor and for the various other needs of the Church.

Jesus does not need our suffering, but we can unite in His suffering. When a father is fixing the lawnmower he can invite his son or daughter by asking them to get a tool from the garage for him. He really does not need his children to do the actual repair but he invites them to help him in the project. The same with Jesus. He provides the opportunity for us to suffer in union with him.

Simcha Fisher wrote an article for the National Catholic Register with the catchy title "Suck It Up Versus Offering It Up". One of my granddaughters was complaining one time about some injustice. A friend of her mother's said to the granddaughter "Suck it up, butter cup". It has reference to phrases like live with it, stuff it, deal with it. Or, shove it down and keep it in. Offering it up, on the other hand, turns the positive attention upward to God as a loving act.

There is a story of a priest who asked Pope John Paul II, "Holy Father please pray for my knee." It is said the Pope slapped the priest and told him "Don't waste your suffering, put it to work for salvation."

"Offering it up" is not just some pious platitude but it is an opportunity to raise our sacrifices up to God for the merit of others in the world, the souls in Purgatory, for ourselves and the sinful world we live in.

We now turn to Lent that calls for the practice of making sacrifices. The big difference is that there is always an open season for offering sacrifices up. You can do it anytime.

Lent

Lent is a forty-day period to prepare us for Easter. "By the solemn forty days of Lent the Church unites herself each year to the mystery of Jesus in the desert" (CCC 540). The number 40 is found many times in the Bible. Moses was on Mt. Sinai forty days fasting from food and water in the presence of God. The Hebrews wandered in the desert for forty years. Rain came down for forty days and nights causing the Great Flood. Elijah walked for 40 days and nights to Mt. Horeb. It took 40 days to prepare Jacob's body for burial.

The plan for a 40-day Lenten period came about around the time of the Counsel of Nicea in 325 AD. The underpinnings of the creation of Lent came from both Jesus' 40 days in the desert and what Luke reported Jesus declaring "If anyone wishes to come after me, he must deny himself and take up his cross daily and follow me (Luke 9:23).

Denial of a worldly-centered self is a key directive that symbolizes the whole purpose of Lent.

The Church's prescribed sacrifices are fasting and the abstinence from meat on Ash Wednesday and Fridays. A little boy was riding in a car with his mother and father. He heard his mother tell his father, "Remember Lent starts tomorrow and we need to begin fasting." The little boy said "Yippee, we can go to McDonalds tomorrow." His father told him fasting does not mean fast food. The little boy responded, "I'm all confused."

My daughter in high school had big plans to go to Key West with some friends during Lent on spring break. Before she left, a friend that was not able to go asked her, "What are you giving up for Lent?" My daughter replied, "I'm giving up meat." The friend said, "Don't you know that fish is meat?" The daughter showing her naiveté bought the idea that fish is meat and did not enjoy eating any fish that she loved so much and is so special in Key West. Later when she discovered that she had been hoodwinked by her friend, she now knows that fish is not meat.

The famous Fat Tuesday or Mardi Gras in French takes place in New Orleans the day before Ash Wednesday. It is a wild and crazy festival time marked by parties, costumes, parades, a lot of drinking, and wearing colorful beads. It has a bacchanalian festival atmosphere about it. The Fat Tuesday name appears to come from the tradition of a pre-Lent feast of eggs, milk, cheese, and meat and other fatty foods.

Lent provides a serious opportunity to examine one's life from a moral and spiritual standpoint. Fasting and abstinence is just a starting point. We can "give up" alcohol, smoking, eating sweets, snacks, shopping, playing video games and watching a favorite TV show. But we can also do positive things that we promised ourselves to start to do or do more of. Examples can include praying a daily rosary, saying positive uplifting comments to others, contributing more in the collection basket and really trying to listen better to our spouse and children.

There are a number of additional opportunities for making Lent more meaningful in our lives.

• Penance

• Almsgiving

• Adoration of the Blessed Sacrament

• Attending the Stations of the Cross

• Going to Mass during the week

The spirit of Lent is meant to empower us to orient our lives toward God during this special time of the year. It is known in Old English and Old Dutch as "spring season". It provides a nice connection to something called spring cleaning. Spring cleaning is the practice of thoroughly cleaning a house in the springtime. Lent provides a great opportunity to do spring cleaning of our spiritual lives.

The Communion of Saints

The concept of and belief in the Communion of Saints is included in both the Nicene Creed and Apostles' Creed. The basis for the Communion of Saints flows from this Bible passage "Now you are Christ's body, and individually parts of it"

(1 Corinthians 12:27).

Christ is the head of the mystical body that includes the following faithful souls, both living and dead:

The Church Militant-we Christians on earth who must battle with the evil in the world

The Church Penitent-the souls in Purgatory

The Church Triumphant-the Saints in heaven

Each group of Christians is in a mystical union with Christ and share in the benefits of interaction with one another and with Him. We sojourners or pilgrims on earth can pray to the saints in heaven and they also pray for us. We pray for the souls in Purgatory.

All are "saints" even those that are going through purification in Purgatory who someday will be welcomed into heaven. Those in heaven are already saints. We are saints "in the making" and look to that time when we are among those saints that "go marching in." Oh, I so want to be in that number …

Now let us consider the future saints who are in
Purgatory.

The Church Penitent-the Holy Souls in Purgatory

Some refer to them as The Church Suffering. We begin with the good news. The souls in Purgatory are destined for Heaven sometime in the future. While in Purgatory they undergo suffering to spiritually cleanse their souls that some saintly visionaries describe as a horrific burnishing process. Some authors claim Purgatory is an actual place while others say it is a state of conscious awareness of the sadness and sorrow of being separated from God. In either case, several authors have described the purpose of Purgatory is when or where "every trace of attachment to evil must be eliminated, every imperfection of the soul corrected" (Pope John Paul II). Nothing unclean can enter Heaven.

The length of time one spends in Purgatory is related to the person's sinfulness. Dante's Purgatorio is the second part of his Divine Comedy. He visits seven levels or terraces on his climb up the Mountain of Purgatory. Each terrace is connected to one of the seven capital or deadly sins. Pride is at the first terrace for the most serious sin while Lust is at the seventh terrace.

Saint Faustina visited Purgatory guided by her guardian angel.

" ...I saw my Guardian Angel, who ordered me to follow him. In a moment I was in a misty place full of fire in which there was a great crowd of suffering souls. They were praying fervently, but to no avail, for themselves;

only we can come to their aid. The flames, which were burning them, did not touch me at all. My Guardian Angel did not leave me for an instant. I asked these souls what their greatest suffering was. They answered me in one voice that their greatest torment was longing for God. I saw Our Lady visiting the souls in Purgatory. The souls call Her "The Star of the Sea". She brings them refreshment. I wanted to talk with them some more, but my Guardian Angel beckoned me to leave. We went out of that prison of suffering. [I heard an interior voice which said] 'My mercy does not want this, but justice demands it. Since that time, I am in closer communion with the suffering souls.'" (Diary, 20). The interior voice was Jesus'.

Several of the famous saints recounted visits, with God's permission, from holy souls in Purgatory. They include St Lidwinia, St. Catherine of Genoa and St Padre Pio. The purpose of the visits in each case was to ask the saint to offer Masses, prayers and sacrifices to relieve the soul's suffering. We have learned that one of their greatest fears is to be forgotten.

We lift out the phrase from St. Faustina that "They were praying fervently, but to avail, for themselves, only we can come to their aid." We can assist them by means of our prayers and offering up our sacrifices on their behalf. In the book Hungry Souls there are many stories of souls that God allows to reach out to the living asking for prayers and sacrifices to relieve their suffering and to warn us to change our lives to save us from hell and shorten our time in Purgatory. The visits often leave evidence of the encounters like hand prints burned into clothing and in books, for example, or next to specific passages in the Bible. The burn marks cannot be explained by natural means. Many of these signs can be found in the "Museum of Purgatory" in Rome.

We are called to "offer up" our prayers, sufferings and works for the poor souls in Purgatory. One nice benefit we can receive in return is, once they are in Heaven, they can now pray for us. Amen.

The Church Militant-We Are the Living

Militant means we must battle against all the evil in the world and fight using the spiritual armor St Paul describes in Ephesians 6:11 to defend our faith in God. We are also challenged by Jesus' second great commandment to "love your neighbor as yourself". The Corporal Works of Mercy list some of our neighbor's needs. We are to reach out to the hungry, the thirsty, those without shelter, the sick, the prisoners, we are to give alms to the poor and bury the dead. The seven Spiritual Works of Mercy include:

- Counseling the Doubtful

- Instructing the Ignorant

- Admonishing the Sinner

- Comforting the Sorrowful

- Forgiving Injuries

- Bearing Wrongs Patiently

- Praying for the Living and the Dead

We can examine the list of these spiritual actions to recall when we have reached out to a neighbor who needed our help or when we grew stronger within our self.

In a NCIS television episode, Jimmy Palmer asked his colleagues for a donation to his favorite charity to build a playground for disabled children. When he approached Nick Torres, Nick said he had no cash, so he made his donation electronically. When Palmer returned later, he hugged Nick due to the size of the donation. Nick was flabbergasted. He then learned that he had forgotten to insert a decimal point that made the gift $500 instead of the intended $50. He had planned to set aside the $450 toward purchasing a motorcycle for himself. He did his best to correct the mistake. But when Jimmy took Nick on a tour of the playground, he was amazed to see how much the kids with disabilities were enjoying the playground. Nick's heart melted and he decided his gift of $500 was well deserved.

Nick's story is one example of how a change in one's attitude can lead to reaching out to those in need.

A friend was asked to give a talk at a retreat. She began the talk by claiming that the chore she hated the most was doing the laundry. The children left their dirty clothes all over the place and her husband dropped one of his socks in one place and she had to search for the other one usually hidden under the bed. This one time when she was moaning and groaning about having to do the laundry, she suddenly received this insight. If she hadn't been blessed with a wonderful husband and three lovely children she wouldn't need to do all that laundry. Immediately, she thanked God for blessing her with her family as she took on a whole different attitude toward doing the laundry from that time on.

Let me share my story of how offering it up changed my life. I have discovered along the way that personal power and control can be my biggest enemy. It has taken those times when I finally "gave in" that have taught me that surrender was the smart and the best way to go. I offer this example. I have been a diehard fan of the Cincinnati Bengals football team as long as they have existed. In 1989 my wife Pat asked me to go to a parish retreat at St. Patrick Church. It would start on a Saturday morning and end with a closing Mass on Sunday evening. The retreat was on the exact same weekend as the Super Bowl. What's more, my beloved Cincinnati Bengals were in that Super Bowl! It was their first time in the Super Bowl. I did everything I could to talk my way out of going to that retreat. "Why would they ever schedule a retreat that was on a Super Bowl Sunday in the first place?" I begged, pleaded and argued that there was no way I was going to give up watching my Bengals in the Super Bowl. But God bless her, Pat never argued or pressured me to go other than saying "It would be good to support the retreat team" or "It would be nice if we could go together".

No matter what reason I offered she stuck to her guns in a calm, prayerful manner. In desperation I finally said in a huff something like, "All right, I'll go but only to please you." As the good Lord would have it, the retreat absolutely changed my life. It gifted me with such a spiritually powerful experience that it had to be very similar to what the apostles must have felt in the upper room on Pentecost. It was an absolute inrush of God's grace. It's been said, "Life is what happens to you while you're busy making other plans." I wasn't looking for a "personal God touch" and almost did my best to miss out on that marvelous event.

Indeed, God works in very mysterious ways and when we relax and give in (call it "surrender"), the rewards can be stupendous. Take a moment to recall those times in your life when you gave up something that you wanted very much as a sign of love for an "other" and were blessed with results.

We are called to be militants in facing the evil in the world we live in. Let us examine the present state of the world and how our prayers, sacrifices and good works are so necessary in doing our part to make the world a better place for all our "neighbors" in the world.

Offering Up Suffering

Suffering can be a powerful sacrifice when offered up. God does not need our suffering but it is a loving way to thank, honor and praise him for his great goodness. Just as we can be presented the opportunity to select which charity we want to make a donation to; we can designate who the suffering is for. We can offer it for our self, our "neighbor", the souls in Purgatory or to the Immaculate Heart of Mary for the conversion of sinners and for the whole world. And, it can be a wonderful action step in growing spiritually.

Most people understand the meaning of suffering. The typical association is physical pain that hurts or causes irritation. For some people, the suffering comes from the "loss" of somebody they love, maybe a job or something else of importance to them.

Everybody suffers some loss in their lives. As somebody put it, "Suffering is a required course, it's not an elective." Like anything in life, we try to understand its whys and wherefores.

Suffering calls us to attention. If we merely treat the symptoms we can miss the underlying meaning. It can be a prompt, nudge or a shove-also known as a "wake-up call"- to move us off of dead-center. Henri Fredric Ariel claimed, "You desire to know the art of living, my friend? It is contained in one phrase: "make use of suffering." Suffering has a way of dramatically forcing us to deal with the deeper issues of life. It drives us to ask big questions like "Why am I here?", "What is the purpose of my life?", "Why is this happening to me?" Suffering seems to have a special ability to show us how much we need one another. It provides the opportunity for us to draw closer to one another and to be mutually strengthened as we face the struggles in life together. As John Donne realized, "No man is an island".

In our modern society, the dominating belief is that the only way to deal with suffering is either "grin and bear it" or put all the effort into treating the symptoms. In our American culture, suffering is something to avoid at all costs. James Davies, a psychologist, commented in Timothy Keller's book, *Walking with God through Pain and Suffering*, that the current cultural treatment belief about suffering is "increasingly trapping us within a worldview that regards all suffering as a purely negative force in our lives." This is very unfortunate because it takes away the responsibility of the sufferer to examine their life and the possible underpinnings of the suffering.

Joni Eareckson Tada claimed that a diving accident when she was seventeen leaving her a quadriplegic in a wheelchair was a "glorious intruder," the best thing that ever happened to her. She believes God used it to get her attention and to direct her thoughts toward Him. However, it took nearly two years before she arrived at that point after suffering through anger, depression, bitterness, suicidal thoughts, and religious doubts.

If you throw a stone in a pond it can cause concentric circles to travel outward affecting everything along its path. Call it the ripple effect. Similarly, everything we do affects other people in our lives and their reactions in turn affect others. Every action causes a reaction. In short, the choices one makes can have far-reaching consequences. They can turn out good or bad.

Because the ripple of sin or of good deeds can affect more than you and me, each of us carries within us the capacity to change the world in small ways for better or worse. Prayers and suffering offered up for others causes a ripple effect that can be felt by them not only many miles away but supernaturally beyond time and space. One might say they travel through a magical, mystery pathway.

The World Needs Our Prayers, Sacrifices and Good Works

Why does the world need them? It seems every day we are bombarded by news of politicians, entertainers and even teachers being accused of sexual harassment and depravity. It's no big surprise that incest has violated the sanctity of children since the beginning of time. And, more predators are coming out of the woodwork than we could have ever imagined. We now must worry about neighbors, swimming coaches, dance instructors, priests and ministers, the camp counselor, the Little League Coach, the baby sitter, etc. Who can we trust? The answer seems to be, nobody.

With the advent of the Internet, sexual predators now can even infiltrate the sanctity of our homes and entice naïve children to enter their evil spider webs. Child pornography is becoming a much bigger scourge, and more and more kids are being sucked into prostitution and sex trafficking. Sexting looms as a dangerously new threat to child sexual morality and personal integrity.

Much of the moral and social decay can be charged to the erosion of the traditional American family. Statistics bear out some of the likely reasons for this drastic change in family composition.

Dennis Prager claims in the article "America's Accelerating Decay" that "Nearly half (48 percent) of American children are born to a mother who is not married. Forty-three percent of American children live without a father in the home. About 50 percent of Americans over 18 are married, compared with 72 percent in 1960. Americans are having so few children that the fertility rate fell to a record low 62.0 births per 1,000 women in 2016. And in an increasing number of states, there are now more deaths than births."

We can never forget that our children are targeted by Satan. Anthony Comstock claimed, "The world is the devil's hunting-ground, and children are his choicest game." What better way to devastate human morale and retaliate against Jesus by preying on children that Jesus loves so very much.

Then there are the terrorists and madmen who are killing many people. The Las Vegas shooter killed 58 people, 20 children were murdered at Sandy Hook School and 28 people were mowed down in a Baptist church in Sutherland Springs, Texas as examples. There are at least ten armed conflicts going on every day in the world. And, we are now, as usual, faced with the dangerous threat of nuclear annihilation between the United States and North Korea, or possibly China, or even Russia.

There is an epidemic of drug related deaths in America. The number of drug overdose deaths among 15-to-19-year-olds keeps rising according to the report from the U.S. Centers for Disease Control and Prevention. New synthetic designer drugs like "flakka" are causing massive problems. The new drugs tend to be cheaper, easy to obtain and cause many of the users to show extremely bazaar and dangerous behavior.

In 1917, Our Lady appeared in Fatima, Portugal for six consecutive months, from May to October, to three shepherd children: Lucia, Francisco and Jacinta. They were nine, seven and six years-old respectively. The overriding message from Our Lady of Fatima was that the children and all of us need to pray fervently and offer up many sacrifices for the conversion of sinners. If we do not, as she prophesized, more wars will come (World War II), there will be persecution of the Church, many good Christian people will be martyred (e.g., like those killed by ISIS) and the Pope will have much to suffer (Pope John Paul II was shot on May 13, 1981). The Church and the pope presently are buried in a terrible sexual abuse scandal and accusations of apostacy.

At her final apparition, as Our Lady prophesized, there was a "miracle of the sun" that was witnessed by seventy-thousand people. Pope Benedict XVI said that the Fatima apparitions were "without a doubt, the most prophetic of all modern apparitions."

Many of the prophecies have already come true. There are other ones that loom for the future that appear apocalyptic in nature. We have been warned to seriously consider offering up our prayers, sacrifices and good works to convert sinners and as reparation for the many offenses to God. We need to do our part to save the world.

My Experience with Suffering

In my book *Suffering and Spirituality: My Story*, I describe some of the suffering in my life. There are many people who have suffered longer and more severely than I have. I would lose badly in comparison to those that have suffered so much. Most Christians immediately will offer Jesus Christ as someone who experienced horrific suffering ending in a torturous death for the salvation of mankind.

I certainly have had my share of life events to suffer through. Tragic death of my father when I was ten, stricken with polio at age twenty-two, then faced with colon cancer, and to top it off-having a successful business raided and shut down by the FBI due to malfeasance by a colleague in a partner organization. This seems to me an unusual combination of opportunities for suffering. But a more recent event provided an instantaneous sucker punch right in my gut. You never know how intense the suffering will be and how long it will last. I had to surrender my driver's license. That had a devastating impact on me. Suffering hurts. It's painful whether it is physical, mental, emotional or spiritual.

Where has all this suffering brought me to this point? I frequently find myself asking if the suffering I experience is an opportunity to "offer it up" or use pain medication to make it to just go away. The very fact I am asking that question tells me that I seem to be growing spiritually at least a little bit.

A short time after publishing *Suffering and Spirituality: My Story*, one early morning when I was very groggy from lack of sleep and the after-effects from Advil taken for pain, I suddenly received an insight that I know did not from me. The message was that God was pleased with the book and wanted me to write more on the topic of suffering and spirituality. Thus, this little book.

Little did I know that it would lead to a deeper and more demanding experience with suffering. One morning when the wound care specialist at my home took the wraps off my leg, we discovered that my whole right leg was bright red from cellulitis. I immediately went to the emergency room for treatment and finally 38 days later I was discharged to go home. Things got progressively worse while in the hospital. Following treatment for the cellulitis, my bowels stopped working, then I went into A Fib and later was diagnosed with C diff.

My wife Pat, a retired physical therapist, uses a formula to determine how much loss of strength comes from lying in a hospital bed. The estimate is that the patient loses between 3 to 5 percent each day. That means I lost an average of 4 percent times 18 days in the hospital totaling seventy-two percent of my strength. After twenty days of physical therapy at a rehabilitation center and therapy in my home I recovered the lost strength and endurance.

I want to share how I found "offering it up" to be very helpful during those 38 days with some examples.

During therapy I used an upper cycle for twenty minutes each day. Each time I would offer it up for a specific person or the souls in Purgatory. I was not only increasing my physical strength but also building my spiritual muscle. I was faced with many challenges. One night an aide greeted me with "What do you want?" in a nasty tone of voice. I asked her to change my briefs due to an accident. She turned the call light off, made an about face and left. She never returned. I waited for an hour and a half later until another aide responded to my call light. It was too hard to offer that up.

I did find myself using "offering it up" on other occasions when, for example, the meal tray often did not contain the items I liked which I had selected on my menu order ticket. Waiting patiently for certain things to happen like undue delays before someone came to help me get out of bed, to bring me pain medication, or change painful positions in the bed were other opportunities to "offer it up".

As time went on, I found myself "offering it up" more and more. I recognized the many opportunities I could use to make sacrifices for myself, to God and for others.

There are plenty of opportunities to offer it up. Some preliminary points are:

• Don't pick something that goes against medical advice

• Select something that is easy to do that you are more likely to remember to "offer it up"

• It is very hard to think of offering it up when the pain and suffering are overwhelming

• Place a visual reminder of your plan that is easy to see, for example, on the bathroom mirror or on the dashboard of your car

It is very easy to forget that we have a number of opportunities during the day that we can use for offering it up.

Through repetition comes remembering. I have found the Morning Offering prayer to be very helpful. It includes offering up our "prayer, works, joys and sufferings." At night before going to bed I review how the day went regarding those four offerings in the Morning Offering prayer.

Here is a partial list of some opportunities for offering it up you could consider:

Waiting:

Waiting in the doctor or dentist's office

Waiting in line

Waiting in traffic

Waiting for a repair person to come

Waiting for a check or gift card in the mail

Waiting for a chance to talk

Waiting for the weather to change

Waiting for anything else

Irritations and frustrations:

Children are on your nerves

When feeling sad, depressed, angry, tense, etc.

Too much noise

When you catch yourself doing negative self-talk

When you have to get up and tend to a crying baby or children misbehaving

Certain chores like doing the laundry or mowing the grass-other tasks you do not like to do

Biting your tongue from being overly critical or too judgmental

Feeling hurt, overlooked, not thanked or ignored

Listening to a boring or overly long homily or sermon

Interruption during a favorite TV show or game

This is a relatively short list. I hope you will pick something you can work on. It is very easy in the beginning to forget. That's why it is important to select one that you are more likely to practice "offering it up" to achieve your first success.

Don't get discouraged and keep the visual reminders in easy sight. With time you will build a habit of thinking about the first task you memorized and then you can confidently move onto other ones.

Offering it up is very valuable sacrifice on behalf of the beneficiaries and will make you spiritually stronger.

Epilogue

I am convinced that "offering it up" presents a marvelous opportunity to deny oneself as a gift of sacrifice for ourselves and others. It combines the directives to deny our self-following in the footsteps of Jesus and his command to love your neighbor as yourself.

Prayers, suffering and good works provide a positive ripple effect of love that can be felt by those near and far away even in Purgatory.

Please consider if offering it up would be a good practice for you to incorporate into your spiritual life if you are not presently doing it. I highly recommend it.

Bibliography

Alighieri, Dante. The Divine Comedy: The Complete
Edition Paperback. CreateSpace Independent Publishing
Platform, October 23, 2017.

Catechism of the Catholic Church. U.S. Catholic Church.
Double Day; 2nd edition, March 4, 2003.

Fisher, Simka. "Suck It Up versus Offering It Up".
National Catholic Register, March 9, 2016.

Keller, Timothy. Walking with God through Pain and
Suffering. Penguin Books, New York, 2013.

Kowalska, Maria Faustina. Saint Faustina Diary: Divine
Mercy in My Soul, Marian Press; 3rd edition, February
15, 2005.

Prager, Dennis. "America's Accelerating Decay". The
National Review. April 7, 2015.

The New American Bible, Revised Edition (NABRE).
World Bible Publishing, March 9, 2011.

Timmerman, W. J. Suffering and Spirituality: My Story.
CreateSpace Independent Publishing Platform,
September 6, 2017.

Timmerman, William. America's Children in the 21st
Century-A Call to Action. Outskirts Press, September 21,
2014.

van den Aardweg, Gerald J.M. Hungry Souls:
Supernatural Visits, Messages, and Warnings from
Purgatory. TAN Books, November 1, 2009.

Prayers

Apostles Creed

I believe in God, the Father Almighty, Creator of heaven and earth and in Jesus Christ, His only Son, our Lord; Who was conceived by the Holy Spirit, born of the Virgin Mary, suffered under Pontius Pilate, was crucified, died, and was buried, He descended into hell; the third day He arose again from the dead; He ascended into Heaven, seated at the right hand of God, the Father Almighty, from there He shall come to judge the living and the dead. I believe in the Holy Spirit, the Holy Catholic Church, the communion of saints, the forgiveness of sins, the resurrection of the body, and life everlasting. Amen.

Our Father

Our Father, Who art in Heaven, hallowed be Thy name; Thy Kingdom come, Thy will be done on earth as it is in Heaven. Give us this day our daily bread; and forgive us our trespasses as we forgive those who trespass against us; and lead us not into temptation, but deliver us from evil. Amen.

Glory Be

Glory be to the Father, the Son, and the Holy Spirit. As it was, in the beginning, is now and ever shall be, world without end. Amen.

O My Jesus (The Fatima Prayer)

O my Jesus, forgive us our sins. Save us from the fires of hell. Take all souls into heaven, especially, those most in need of thy mercy. Amen.

Hail Mary

Hail Mary, full of grace, the Lord is with thee, blessed art thou amongst women and blessed is the fruit of thy womb, Jesus. Holy Mary Mother of God, pray for us sinners now and at the hour of our death. Amen.

Hail Holy Queen

Hail Holy Queen, Mother of Mercy, our life our sweetness and our hope. To thee do we cry, poor banished children of Eve; To thee do we send up our sighs, mourning and weeping in this valley of tears. Turn then, most gracious advocate, thine eyes of mercy toward us and after this our exile show unto us the blessed fruit of thy womb, Jesus. O clement, O loving, O sweet Virgin Mary!

Pray for us, O Holy Mother of God That we may be made worthy of the promises of Christ.

Let Us Pray (The Rosary Prayer)

Let us Pray. O God, whose only begotten Son, by His life, death, and resurrection, has purchased for us the rewards of eternal salvation. Grant, we beseech Thee, that while meditating on these mysteries of the most holy Rosary of the Blessed Virgin Mary, that we may imitate what they contain and obtain what they promise, through Christ our Lord. Amen. Most Sacred

Heart of Jesus, have mercy on us. Immaculate Heart of Mary, pray for us.

Other Prayers

The Morning Offering Prayer

"O Jesus, through the Immaculate heart of Mary, and in union with the Holy Sacrifice of the Mass being offered throughout the world, I offer you all my prayers, works, joys and sufferings of this day in reparation for the offenses committed against the Immaculate heart of Mary, for my sins, and the sins of the whole world."

The Memorare Prayer

REMEMBER, O most gracious Virgin Mary, that never was it known that anyone who fled to thy protection, implored thy help, or sought thy intercession was left unaided. Inspired with this confidence, I fly to thee, O Virgin of virgins, my Mother; to thee do I come; before thee I stand, sinful and sorrowful. O Mother of the Word Incarnate, despise not my petitions, but in thy mercy hear and answer me. Amen.

Other Books by the Author

Suffering and Spirituality: My Story

Suffering: It Sucks, It Sanctifies, or What?

Prepare for the Garabandal Warning

Our Lady of Civitavecchia and the Bleeding Statue

Is God Using UFOs?

Mass Murderers and the Seven Deadly Sins

Our Mother Mary's Warnings at Civitavecchia, Akita, Garabandal and Fatima

Why Praying at Noon Is So Important

Your Guardian Angel: Things You Maybe Didn't Know

Holy Face of Jesus Medal

Evil Really Stinks

The Many Wounds Jesus Suffered

The Power of His Holy Face for Your Life

Thanks, God for Those Close Moments

LUST: The Devil's Favorite Sin

The Devil on My Shoulder

Growing Up on Rural Route 2

Sins and God's Warning

What the Angels Have Taught Me

For People Who Are Suffering: A Treasure of Wise Sayings

Goofy Laws Goofy World

I Bet You Are Envious Like I Am

Where the Hell Did "Hell" Go?

The Scary Warning from Garabandal

The Sacred Power of 3 O'clock Prayer

The Spiritual Power of Acronyms Workbook

Spiritual Microchips: How to Access Yours

In 2034 Anti-Christianity Triumphs in America

Am I Crazy or Just Senile?

Who Is "Angel Phanuel"?

America Doesn't Love Children

Can the Devil Read Our Minds?